Partner Read-Alouds

AESOP'S FABLES

11 Leveled Stories to Read
Together for Gaining Fluency & Comprehension

by
Kathryn Wheeler
and Debra Olson Pressnall

Key Education
Carson-Dellosa Publishing Company LLC
Greensboro, North Carolina

www.keyeducationpublishing.com

CONGRATULATIONS ON YOUR PURCHASE OF A KEY EDUCATION PRODUCT!

The editors at Key Education are former teachers who bring experience, enthusiasm, and quality to each and every product. Thousands of teachers have looked to the staff at Key Education for new and innovative resources to make their work more enjoyable and rewarding. Key Education is committed to developing and publishing educational materials that will assist teachers in building a strong and developmentally appropriate curriculum for young children.

PLAN FOR GREAT TEACHING EXPERIENCES WHEN YOU USE EDUCATIONAL MATERIALS FROM KEY EDUCATION

About the Authors

Kathryn Wheeler has worked as a teacher, an educational consultant, and an editor in educational publishing. She has published workbooks, stories, and magazine articles for children. Kate was awarded a Michigan Council for the Arts grant for fiction. She has a B.A. degree in English from Hope College. Kate lives in Michigan with her husband, Don.

Debra Olson Pressnall has been an editor, writer, and product developer in the educational publishing field for over 20 years. She earned her bachelor of science degree in elementary education from Concordia College (Minnesota) and then spent 12 years as an educator in elementary classrooms before entering the supplemental education publishing field. She has authored dozens of classroom teaching aids as well as 12 books for teachers, including Key Education's *Lively Literacy & Music Activities* and *Sound Out and Sort*. Debra has been the recipient of two Directors' Choice Awards, two *Creative Child Magazine* Awards, and a Parents' Choice Honors award. She lives in Minnesota with her very supportive husband, Steve, and son, Brandon.

Credits
Content Editor and Layout Design: Debra Olson Pressnall
Copy Editor: Karen Seberg
Inside Illustrations: Julie Anderson
Cover Design: Annette Hollister-Papp
Cover Illustrations: JJ Rudisill
Cover Photographs: © Shutterstock

Key Education
An imprint of Carson-Dellosa Publishing LLC
PO Box 35665
Greensboro, NC 27425 USA
www.keyeducationpublishing.com

ISBN 978-1-602681-20-0
01-335118091

Table of Contents

Building Fluency & Comprehension Skills with Fables

If your students can decode words and recognize many high-frequency words, but read passages word-for-word with monotone voices, there are strategies that can help them become fluent readers. Perhaps you are asking, what is fluency? Is it more than just reading a certain number of words in a passage accurately per minute? When students read aloud effortlessly with expression, comprehension, and accuracy and at a proper rate, they have become fluent readers. Fluency instruction is the bridge from phonics and sight-word practice to comprehension. In *Partner Read-Alouds: Aesop's Fables*, familiar and well-loved stories have been retold with simple sentence structures to help struggling and reluctant readers gain fluency. Accompanying each story are comprehension activities to build understanding of story elements. *To find out the readability of each story, which was determined by using the Spache Formula, please refer to the Table of Contents.*

Enjoy these new versions of time-honored fables as you guide your students down the path toward fluency!

Strategies for Improving Fluency

- **Select stories that draw students into seeing mental images when reading them.** Aesop's fables are stories that have had an appeal to children for centuries. We don't know very much about the historic Aesop, but we can gather that he was a tactful person with a good sense of humor. This fact is displayed through his use of animal characters, who teach the lessons embedded in the story without offending human listeners. His humor is evident in the many complicated situations in which his characters find themselves.

  The stories in *Partner Read-Alouds: Aesop's Fables* can become a natural springboard for talking about positive character traits like caring for others, thinking before you act, liking yourself the way that you are, and being truthful.

- **Model for students how to read a passage fluently and how to comprehend while reading.** It is helpful for struggling readers to hear how your voice changes in pitch and conveys emotion, how you pause at the end of sentences, and how you cluster words in meaningful ways. To introduce each story in this resource, have students listen and read along silently while you read aloud the first page. Then, follow up with a discussion: point out punctuation marks in the text, talk about how the tone of your voice conveyed emotion, explain new vocabulary, and so on. This introductory session is also a perfect opportunity to demonstrate how a reader thinks about what is being read. See the section Thinking About Each Story for additional tips.

- **Have students read aloud the same story several times to polish expressive reading skills and to recognize more words automatically.** These can be large- or small-group choral reading, echo reading, readers' theater techniques, and paired reading experiences. (See the next page for additional suggestions.) The funny dialogue and repeated thoughts in each story helps to make the experience enjoyable for struggling readers.

Maximizing In-Class and Out-of-Class Reading-Aloud Experiences

Keeping students engaged and enjoying the read-aloud sessions is very important. They can lose interest if the same approach is used time after time. So here are some ideas for you to consider:

• **Dramatize Passages with a Theatrical Flair!** Try using different voices for characters as you read aloud a story. There will be lots of smiles in your classroom if you do! And, you might notice children trying their best to be just as dramatic when reading with their partners. It certainly makes the characters come to life!

• **Plan Choral Readings:** Having everyone read at the same time supports those children who are uncomfortable reading aloud. During these sessions, it is important **not** to draw attention to individual children by asking them to read a short passage for the entire class. All of your students must listen carefully to read as "one voice" with you as the leader and not be nervous about the possibility of being singled out to read by themselves.

• **Assign Parts Like a Readers' Theater:** The stories in this book can also be modified easily into a Readers' Theater script. If available, use interactive white board software and project a copy of a story for the class to read. Work through the story and highlight those parts in yellow that can be handled by a narrator. Assign a reader for that role. Designate small groups of children as Reader 1 or Reader 2. Then, let students "perform" the story using their best theatrical "one voice."

• **Encourage Reading with a Buddy in Class and out of Class:** In addition to what takes place during your guided-reading sessions, it is important for children to read aloud a story with a partner to strengthen their fluency skills. A lot of practice is needed before students can read smoothly and with expression. By having a partner listen to them read designated parts of a story, struggling readers can receive immediate feedback and encouragement. They also sharpen their auditory skills by listening to someone else read as they follow along with the text. The benefit is that students recognize more words automatically and gain awareness of when to pause. *Use the parent letters on page 6 to seek additional support from families.*

Thinking About Each Story

Boosting reading comprehension skills can be approached in two different ways when using the stories in this book.

Guided-Reading Sessions: Introduce a fable by reading the first page aloud for students. Then, stop at the end of that page and ask students to predict what they think will happen next. Invite them to discuss their predictions with partners before telling their ideas to the class. This is also a perfect opportunity for students to analyze story elements and explain what they have learned so far about the main character. Then, record your students' observations about the story on your white board for future discussions. If interested, read aloud the second page to find out if your students' predictions were accurate. Pause occasionally and share your thoughts about the story by "thinking out loud," telling the class any questions you might have. Explain how good readers have a stream of mental questions that are answered as they read a passage.

Postreading Activities: Included for each story are two reading activity sheets that target specific comprehension skills. It is recommended that students complete one of the activity pages at the end of each partner read-aloud session. The following skills are addressed through these activities:

• recalling story details
• sequencing story events in proper order
• using vocabulary
• identifying cause-and-effect relationships
• explaining the main character's problem and how it was solved
• comparing and contrasting characters' traits
• making an inference
• drawing conclusions
• writing a fable

Dear Parents,

During the school year, students in your child's class will be reading out loud to improve their reading fluency. Perhaps you are asking, what is fluency? Take a moment to recall your own experiences when you needed to read a selection out loud. Did you think about the context of the passage and watched for punctuation marks while conveying emotion with your voice and reading the words in meaningful groupings? This is reading fluency!

At certain times, your child will bring home an Aesop's fable to share with you. I am inviting you to help your child with this assignment by being a "reading buddy." Please make these reading experiences enjoyable for your child. If your child mispronounces a word while reading aloud, use these strategies:

• Wait to see what your child does before correcting the error.
• Offer clues to help your child figure out the word.
• If the first two strategies are not effective, then tell your child the word.

By having your child read the story aloud several times, the number of words that are recognized automatically will increase. If certain words are troublesome, it is helpful to print the sentences or phrases that contain those words on index cards and have your child practice reading aloud that text separately. Make it fun!

If you have any questions about these reading assignments, please contact me.

Sincerely,

Dear Parents,

In class, your child has been reading aloud the attached story with a partner to become a more fluent reader.

Would you have a few minutes to be your child's "reading buddy"? Let your child choose one of the parts, giving you the remaining role in the script. Then, read the story together out loud. And, for sure, use your most expressive voice to make this storytelling time a pleasant experience and a lot of fun! Repeated readings of the story are always encouraged as well.

Finally, please write a brief message on the back of this paper about the reading session and the progress your child is making. Return this paper by _____.

Thank you for assisting your child with this reading assignment.

Sincerely,

_____ and I have read the story together.

_____
Parent signature

Background

This story is based on the Aesop fable "The Fox and the Goat." The original moral of this story is "Do not trust the advice of someone in trouble." It also illustrates the adage, "Look before you leap."

Demonstrating Fluent Reading

Model fluent reading for your students by reading aloud the first page. After the reading, ask students to predict what might happen next in the story.

Highlight a short section of dialogue, such as the opening exchange between Speedy and Tricky. Ask pairs of students to give a dramatic reading of the dialogue during guided reading time. Suggest that they try different inflections and voices for the lines (*you will probably want to model this for them first*).

Also, during this instruction time, pair students and have them read the selected dialogue at least four times. In order for this not to become tiresome for the class, have the pairs spread out in the room. Then, circulate among the students to listen to the readings of each pair.

Prereading Activity: Building Vocabulary

Before reading the story, review these vocabulary words with your students:

sparrow	darted	thirsty	trot
finally	shady	scrambled	bleat

Reading with a Buddy

Pair students and have them be partners.

Day 1: Let students read aloud the story with "one voice" in unison to work on word recognition and fluency skills.

Day 2: Direct students to choose a part and read the story aloud again.

Day 3: Have students switch parts and reread the story to each other.

At the end of the third day, let your students show off how fluently they can read this story by taking home a copy of it. Encourage each student to read it aloud with a parent or another adult and then return the signed parent letter. (See page 6.)

Postreading Activities: Comprehension

Day 1: After they read the script aloud with partners, have the student pairs discuss what they liked about the story. Let them figure out the moral or lesson that the story conveys.

Day 2: Have students determine cause and effect and list synonyms for the words *dark* and *cool* to finish the activity on page 10.

Day 3: Direct students to complete the activity Thinking About the Story on page 11 by analyzing the characters' traits and actions and writing about the lesson learned by Greta Goat.

Character Education Connection

Discuss the moral of the story.
- What does it mean to "look before you leap"?
- Why shouldn't Greta have trusted Tricky?
- Who was the friend that Greta could trust?
- Who are your trusted friends?

Science Connection

In Aesop's fables, the fox is cunning and tricky. What real-life qualities do foxes have that led Aesop to this portrayal? Have your students research facts in books or on the Internet about foxes.

– The Fable –
A Well of Trouble

Reader 1 "Hot, hot, hot!" complained Tricky Fox. He walked slowly. His feet hurt. He had spent the whole, hot day looking for water.

Reader 2 Speedy Sparrow darted down. "Tricky, you look tired! You look thirsty!" The little bird flew around the fox's head.

Reader 1 Tricky said, "I am looking for water. Can you tell me where to find it?"

Reader 2 Speedy flew up to the tree before she answered. She knew that Tricky was full of tricks. He might even try to eat her if she got too close!

Reader 2 "Keep going down that path," said Speedy. "There's a deep well at the end." Then, she flew away.

Reader 1 "A well!" said Tricky. "What good news! I am such a lucky fox." Tricky started to trot. The sun was hot. Tricky knew that soon he would get a cold drink of water from the well.

Reader 1 At the end of the path was the well. "Hooray!" said Tricky. He looked over the edge. "Oh, no!" said the fox. "It is too deep. I cannot reach the water."

Reader 2 He tried to lean down into the dark, cool well. Suddenly, there was a huge SPLASH! Tricky had fallen into the well.

Reader 1 "HELP!" cried Tricky. "Help! Help! HELP!" But, nobody could hear him.

Reader 2 Tricky took a long drink of water. He was standing in the water at the bottom of the well. After the hot sun, it felt good. But Tricky knew he was in trouble. He also knew that he had played tricks on a lot of animals. None of them would want to come close enough to help him.

Reader 1 Tricky thought and thought. Then, he waited. Finally, he heard a voice. It was Greta Goat. "Hello, Greta!" Tricky called.

Reader 2 Greta looked over the edge. "Tricky! What are you doing down there?"

Reader 1 "Oh," said Tricky. "It's such a hot day. This well is very cool and shady. So I jumped in. It's nice down here."

Reader 2 "I see," said Greta. She started to leave.

Reader 1 "And," Tricky called, "the water here is the best in the woods! Did you know that? I have never tasted water this sweet. Why, it almost tastes like . . ." Tricky thought hard, " . . . it almost tastes like HAY."

Reader 2 Greta looked down again. "Really?" she asked. "That sounds great." She looked at the water. Then, she jumped down. She drank for a long time.

Reader 2 "This is good water!" said Greta. "I'm not sure it tastes like hay. But, it sure tastes good on this hot day!" She looked up to the top of the well. "Now, how do we get out?"

Reader 1 Tricky smiled. "I will show you!" He jumped onto Greta's back. Next, he climbed up to her head. He scrambled up her long horns. Then, Tricky jumped up and climbed out of the well.

Reader 2 "But, how do I get out?" Greta called.

Reader 1 "You will have to find your own way out," called Tricky. "Goodbye!" And, the fox was gone.

Reader 2 Greta started to bleat. "Help, help!" she called.

Reader 1 At last, her friend the farmer found her. "Greta, you silly goat! How did you get down there?" He ran to get help. The farmer and his helpers lifted Greta out of the well.

Reader 2 "I am a silly goat!" thought Greta that night. She ate her sweet hay. She chewed and thought. "But now I see two things," Greta told herself. "I will never trust that fox again. And, I will always look before I leap!"

Name: _____

A Well of Trouble: Checking for Details

Directions: A **cause** makes something happen. An **effect** happens as a result of a cause. Write the cause or effect in the blank.

Cause		**Effect**
1. _____ _____	➜	Tricky fell into the well.
2. Greta Goat jumped into the well.	➜	_____ _____
3. _____ _____	➜	Tricky was able to climb out of the well.
4. Greta bleated "Help, help!"	➜	_____ _____

Directions: Read the sentence from the story. What other words could you use to tell about the well? Make a list below.

He tried to lean down into the dark, cool well.

_____

_____

_____

Name:

A Well of Trouble: Thinking About the Story

Directions: Answer each question with a sentence.

1. Write some words that tell about each character's traits.

Tricky Fox: _____

_____

_____

Greta Goat: _____

_____

_____

2. Who was the friend that Greta could trust? Explain.

_____

_____

3. What lesson did Greta learn?

_____

_____

Try This! What does it mean for you to "look before you leap"? Explain your answer on another sheet of paper.

Background
This story is based on the Aesop fable "The Peacock," or "The Peacock's Tail." There are several versions of the moral for this story, but one is "Be careful what you wish for."

Demonstrating Fluent Reading
Model fluent reading for your students by reading aloud the first page. After the reading, ask students to predict what might happen next in the story.

Select portions of the text to perform as a choral reading during guided reading time. This story has three sections that lend themselves to choral reading because of the emotional "build" from one repeated word to the next. They are the two sections where Sidney says, "I wish! I wish! I WISH!" and the section where Speedy repeats "Wow!" as he beholds Sidney's appearance. Work on these sections first. Encourage students to come up with a pattern of rising voices and exclamations to use for all three sections. Then, have everyone read the story out loud together.

Prereading Activity: Building Vocabulary
Before reading the story, review these vocabulary words with your students:

oak	feathers	pond	mirror
peacock	proudly	gust	self

Reading with a Buddy
Pair students and have them be partners.

Day 1: Let students read aloud the story with "one voice" in unison to work on word recognition and fluency skills.

Day 2: Direct students to choose a part and read the story aloud again.

Day 3: Have students switch parts and reread the story to each other.

At the end of the third day, let your students show off how fluently they can read this story by taking home a copy of it. Encourage each student to read it aloud with a parent or another adult and then return the signed parent letter. (See page 6.)

Postreading Activities: Comprehension
Day 1: After they read the script aloud with partners, have the student pairs discuss what they liked about the story. Let them figure out the moral or lesson that the story conveys.

Day 2: Have students work on page 15 by finishing the sentences and by filling in a comparison chart.

Day 3: Direct students to complete the activity Thinking About the Story on page 16 by analyzing story elements and identifying the lesson learned by Sidney.

Character Education Connection
Discuss the moral of the story.
- Have you ever wanted something very badly and then gotten it and were disappointed?
- What kinds of things do you wish for? Do you think your wishes will come true?

Social Studies Connection
The peacock is a symbol in a number of different cultures. The ancient Greeks talked about peacocks in their myths and plays—which is where Aesop heard of them. In medieval Europe, peacocks were both eaten at banquets and kept as beautiful pets. The peacock is also the national bird of India. Make a bulletin board display about peacocks.

– The Fable –
A Big Wish

Reader 1 A sparrow named Sidney lived in the woods. Sidney was happy. He had a little nest high up in an oak tree. He loved to fly from one tall tree to another. He loved to sit on the roof of a house with other sparrows and look at the world. He loved the feeling of the wind in his feathers as he flew.

Reader 2 Then one day, Sidney went to the pond for a drink of water. It was a still day. The water was like a mirror. Sidney saw himself.

Reader 1 "Oh, dear!" he cried. "I am so ugly! I am gray like the dirt. I am brown like the twigs. My tail is short! My wings are small! I never knew that I looked like this!"

Reader 2 Sidney hid his head under his wing and cried.

Reader 2 For weeks he stayed away from the other sparrows. He felt too bad to go home at night to his little nest. He sat all day and all night on the trunk of a fallen tree.

Reader 1 Then one night, he cried, "How I wish I was beautiful! I wish I had long feathers! I wish I was a pretty color! I wish, I wish, I WISH!"

Reader 2 Sidney wished so hard that his wish came true. The next morning when he woke up, he felt different. He went to the pond and looked. Sidney was a peacock!

Reader 2 He had long feathers that trailed behind him. He could open his tail like a huge fan. He was blue and green. He shone in the sun.

Reader 1 "Hooray! How happy I am!" said Sidney.

Reader 1 Sidney went off to find his friends. The first friend he saw was Speedy Sparrow. Speedy was flying high above the woods. "Speedy!" called Sidney. "Come here!"

Reader 2 Speedy dove down to the ground. Her beak dropped open. "Sidney, is that you?" she asked. She looked at Sidney. "Wow!"

Reader 1 "It is me!" said Sidney. "Look at my feathers!"

Reader 2 "Wow!" said Speedy.

Reader 1 "And look what I can do with my tail!" said Sidney. He opened his tail like a fan. He walked up and down so Speedy could see.

Reader 2 "WOW!" said Speedy. Sidney smiled proudly.

Reader 2 "You have to come with me!" said Speedy. "We need to show everybody. All of the sparrows are meeting on the roof of Farmer Jones's barn. Let's go!"

Reader 2 Speedy took off. A gust of wind pushed her high up in the air. She sped away. Soon, she was a tiny dot in the sky.

Reader 1 Sidney spread his big, heavy wings. He flapped them hard. He tried everything he could think of but he could not follow. "Speedy, wait!" he called. But, Speedy was gone.

Reader 2 Sidney climbed slowly up on the trunk of the fallen tree. "Here I go," he said. "This will be a good test." He flapped his wings. He hopped off the edge. He didn't sail up into the air! He fell to the ground! He knew that he could no longer fly.

Reader 1 "My wings and my tail are too heavy," he thought. "I have these beautiful feathers. But what good are they if I can't fly?

Reader 2 Sidney thought about all the things he loved. Now he could never sit on a roof with his friends and look at the world. He could never go back to his nice little nest at night to rest. He could not fly from one tall tree to another.

Reader 1 Sidney climbed back onto the tree trunk. He wished as hard as he could. "I wish I was a sparrow again! I wish I was brown and gray! I wish, I wish, I WISH!"

Reader 2 The next morning, he hopped to the pond. His wish had come true! He was back to his old self. Sidney flew up into the sky for joy.

Reader 1 "Hooray!" he called. "Look at me! I may be small, brown, and gray. But, I can fly as fast as the wind!" Sidney knew he would never again wish to be changed. He was happy just the way he was.

Name:

Using Vocabulary, Comparing and Contrasting

A Big Wish: Checking for Details

Directions: Use the vocabulary to complete the sentences.

Vocabulary:	feathers	mirror	peacock
	pond	self	sparrow	ugly
	wings	wished	woods	

1. A _____ named Sidney lived in the _____.

2. One day, Sidney went to the _____ for a drink of water.

3. The water was like a _____.

4. Sidney saw himself and thought that he looked _____.

5. The sparrow wished so hard that he became a _____.

6. Sidney's new long _____ trailed behind him.

7. He found out that his _____ and tail were too heavy to fly.

8. Sidney _____ to be his old _____ again.

Directions: Write down the words from the story that tell about the two kinds of birds.

	Sparrow	**Peacock**
Colors		
Tail		
Wings		

KE-804100 © Key Education   -15-   *Partner Read-Alouds: Aesop's Fables*

A Big Wish: Thinking About the Story

Directions: Read the question. Write your answer in the thought bubble.

What do you think Sidney is thinking when he sees his tail feathers for the first time?

Directions: Answer each question with a sentence.

1. What was Sidney's first problem in the story?

_____

_____

2. What was Sidney's second problem?

_____

_____

3. What lesson did Sidney learn?

_____

_____

Try This! Write about a time when you wished for something really hard, but when you got your wish, you were disappointed.

– Teacher's Page –
The Great Peace

Background
This story is based on the Aesop fable "The Cock and the Fox." The original moral for this story is "Liars get caught in their lies."

Demonstrating Fluent Reading
Model fluent reading for your students by reading aloud the first page. After the reading, ask students to predict what might happen next in the story.

Find the paragraph that starts, "Tricky stopped" and read it aloud again. Use this example to show students how to voice a paragraph that explains something. Ask them, "Did you hear how my voice went up on the word *also* when I read, 'But there were also three big dogs'? I did this because it is the inflection that shows why Tricky had to be careful."

Point out to your students that your voice got louder and more tense when you read, "Then, the dogs came running!" Explain that is how you could show that Tricky was in trouble. Let students practice that technique.

Prereading Activity: Building Vocabulary
Before reading the story, review these vocabulary words with your students:

clucked	crowed	feast	henhouse
porch	peace	lambs	greet

Reading with a Buddy
Pair students and have them be partners.

Day 1: Let students read aloud the story with "one voice" in unison to work on word recognition and fluency skills.

Day 2: Direct students to choose a part and read the story aloud again.

Day 3: Have students switch parts and reread the story to each other.

At the end of the third day, let your students show off how fluently they can read this story by taking home a copy of it. Encourage each student to read it aloud with a parent or another adult and then return the signed parent letter. (See page 6.)

Postreading Activities: Comprehension
Day 1: After they read the script aloud with partners, have the student pairs discuss what they liked about the story. Let them figure out the moral or lesson that the fable conveys.

Day 2: Have students make inferences and find the vocabulary words in the word find to finish page 20.

Day 3: Direct students to complete the activity Thinking About the Story on page 21 by analyzing the characters' traits and actions and by identifying the lesson learned.

Character Education Connection
Discuss the moral of the story.
- Why is it always better to tell the truth?
- When somebody lies, is it easy or hard to tell?
- When somebody makes up a story and pretends it is the truth, what can happen?

Math Connection
Make up story problems that relate to "The Great Peace." For example: "If Tricky had tried to steal chickens at Farmer Smith's farm twice before, and now he is trying again, how many times has he tried all together?"

The Great Peace

Reader 1 "I am SO hungry!" said Tricky Fox. He had looked for food all day. It was getting late. "I need dinner!" said Tricky. "I need something good to eat."

Reader 2 Tricky stopped. He was close to Farmer Smith's farm. Tricky was always careful about this farm. There were hens and a fat rooster at the farm. But, there were also three big dogs. Tricky had tried to steal chickens there before. When he tried, the hens clucked and the rooster crowed. Then, the dogs came running!

Reader 1 "I need to think," said Tricky to himself. "I need a good plan. Then, I can catch a hen. Maybe I can even catch that big rooster. I could have a feast tonight!"

Reader 2 Tricky thought and thought. Then, he had an idea.

Reader 2 The fox ran down to the farm. He could not see any hens, but the big rooster was sitting on the roof of the henhouse.

Reader 1 Tricky ran to the henhouse. "Hello, Rooster!" he called. "Come down here and hear the big news!"

Reader 2 The rooster looked down at Tricky. "Thank you. I can hear you fine from here," he said.

Reader 1 "Can you? Because I have very big news!" said Tricky. As he spoke, he looked around. He could see the three dogs. They were lying on the porch. They were asleep.

Reader 2 "Well?" asked the rooster. "What is it?"

Reader 1 "It's about the Great Peace!" said Tricky. He spread out his paws. "All animals are going to be friends from this day forward!"

Reader 2 "Really?" asked the rooster. "Who told you this?"

Reader 1 "Why," said Tricky, "I have just been talking with some little lambs. They are at Farmer Jones's farm. They told me all about it."

Reader 2 "And then, did you eat them?" asked the rooster.

Reader 1 "No, no!" said Tricky. He held up his paws again. He tried to look honest. "The Great Peace means that we are all brothers! I will never eat another animal. Come down here. I will give you a hug!"

Reader 2 The rooster just looked at Tricky. "You are lying," he said.

Reader 1 "No!" said Tricky. "You can trust me. Trust the Great Peace."

Reader 2 "Well, I can try," said the rooster. He started to hop down the roof.

Reader 2 Tricky stood up on his hind legs. "What are you doing?" asked the rooster.

Reader 1 "I am standing up to greet you," said Tricky. "You are my brother now."

Reader 2 The rooster hopped a little closer. Tricky stretched out his paws. "What are you doing now?" asked the rooster.

Reader 1 "I am here to catch you, in case you fall," said Tricky. "That's what brothers do for each other!"

Reader 2 The rooster hopped closer. Tricky reached out to grab the rooster for his dinner. "COCK-A-DOODLE-DOO!" yelled the rooster.

Reader 1 Tricky looked at the porch. The three dogs had jumped up. They started running to the henhouse.

Reader 2 Tricky started to run, too. "Why, Tricky, where are you going?" called the rooster.

Reader 1 "I forgot! I have to be somewhere!" Tricky cried. The dogs started to bark. They ran faster. So did Tricky.

Reader 2 "But, aren't those dogs your brothers?" called the rooster.

Reader 1 "I don't think they have heard about the Great Peace yet!" yelled Tricky. Then, the fox ran into the woods as fast as he could.

Name: _____

Making Inferences, Recognizing Words

The Great Peace: Checking for Details

Directions: Read the question. Write your answer in the bubble.

What do you think Tricky Fox is saying to the rooster?

What do you think the rooster is thinking?

What do you think Tricky is thinking now?

Directions: Read the words in the Word Bank. Circle them in the word find.

Word Bank

animals
brothers
feast
friend
hens
honest
lying
rooster

l	a	h	o	n	e	s	t
y	f	r	i	e	n	d	f
i	p	s	l	y	o	p	e
n	r	u	h	e	n	s	a
g	a	n	i	m	a	l	s
r	o	o	s	t	e	r	t
b	r	o	t	h	e	r	s

Try This! On another paper, use these words in sentences about Tricky Fox.

Name: _____

The Great Peace: Thinking About the Story

Directions:

1. Write some words that tell about each character's traits.

Tricky Fox: _____

_____

The rooster: _____

_____

Directions: Answer each question with a sentence.

2. What was the Great Peace? Why did Tricky want the rooster to believe him?

_____

_____

_____

3. What lesson did you learn from the story?

_____

_____

Tell a Fable! Make up a story about a different animal that must learn the same lesson Tricky learned. Work with a partner and write the fable on paper.

– Teacher's Page –
Donkey Changes Jobs

Background
This story is based on the Aesop fable "The Donkey and the Lapdog." The original moral of this story is "It is better to be satisfied with one's lot than to long for something for which one is not fitted."

Reading with a Buddy
Pair students and have them be partners.

Day 1: Let students read aloud the story with "one voice" in unison to work on word recognition and fluency skills.

Day 2: Direct students to choose a part and read the story aloud again.

Day 3: Have students switch parts and reread the story to each other.

At the end of the third day, let your students show off how fluently they can read this story by taking home a copy of it. Encourage each student to read it aloud with a parent or another adult and then return the signed parent letter. (See page 6.)

Postreading Activities: Comprehension
Day 1: After they read the script aloud with partners, have the student pairs discuss what they liked about the story. Let them figure out the moral or lesson that the fable conveys.

Day 2: Have students recall details and make inferences to finish page 25.

Day 3: Direct students to complete the activity Thinking About the Story on page 26 by analyzing story elements and identifying the lesson learned.

Demonstrating Fluent Reading
Model fluent reading for your students by reading aloud the first page. After the reading, ask students to predict what might happen next in the story.

This is a great story for letting students demonstrate their skill during guided reading time. For example, in the first portion of the story, have one student read the part of Donkey and another student read the part of Goat by changing the tones of their voices.

Find the part in the story where Donkey goes into the farmhouse. You can use great dramatic flair in modeling how to read the "sound effect" words, such as "BANG BANG BANG," "CRASH," and "SMASH!" Students love to make noises like these while reading. Encourage them to read dramatically when working with a buddy.

Character Education Connection
Discuss the moral of the story. A simple rewording of the moral might be, "A good job for one person might not be a good job for someone else."

- Do you have a friend who is good at something you are not?
- Do people have to be good at everything? Why or why not?

Prereading Activity: Building Vocabulary
Before reading the story, review these vocabulary words with your students:

complained	brushes	market	circles
grain	knocked	surprised	crazy

Math Connection
Create simple word problems by using the situations in "Donkey Changes Jobs." For example, "The market is four miles from the farm. How far will Donkey have to pull the cart to bring food to the market and then come back home again?"

– The Fable –

Donkey Changes Jobs

Reader 1 "All day long, it's work, work, work!" Donkey complained.

Reader 2 "But, you have a good life," said Donkey's friend Goat. "Look at your big, warm room in the barn. You have all the food you want. The farmer brushes you every day."

Reader 1 "Every day, I have jobs to do," Donkey pointed out. "I have to pull carts full of wood. I have to take food to the market to sell. I think I need a new job!"

Reader 2 "What job do you want?" asked Goat.

Reader 1 Donkey thought and thought. "I know!" he cried. "I want Pal's job." Pal was the farmer's dog. Pal rode in the cart that Donkey pulled. The farmer carried Pal in his arms. Every night, Pal got to eat with the farmer. Then, he slept on the farmer's lap in front of the fire.

Reader 2 Goat asked, "You want to be a dog?"

Reader 1 Donkey nodded. "Yes," he said. "That's the job for me!"

Reader 2 The next day, Donkey had to pull the cart to the fence. The farmer was fixing the fence. His tools were in the cart.

Reader 1 While Donkey worked, Pal played in the field. He ran in circles. He barked. He chased a rabbit. He chased his tail! "Look at that silly dog," said Donkey. "I need to learn how to act just like him." Donkey watched Pal closely.

Reader 2 Then, Donkey pulled the cart back to the barn. The farmer sat down to rest. Pal ran up and jumped into the farmer's lap. "Good dog!" said the farmer. He petted Pal. Donkey watched Pal closely.

Reader 1 "I need to learn how to do that," Donkey said.

Reader 2 That night the farmer brushed Donkey. He gave Donkey some sweet hay and grain to eat. After the farmer left, Donkey said, "Here is my chance!" He pushed open the barn door. He trotted out into the yard. Then, he went up the steps to the farmer's house.

Reader 1 The door was closed. "How do I get in?" Donkey asked himself. He thought. He remembered the time he watched a guest come to the house. The guest had knocked on the door. "I can do that!" said Donkey. He used his hoof. BANG BANG BANG went his hoof on the door.

Reader 2 The farmer's wife opened the door. "Why, it is the donkey!" she said, surprised. Donkey pushed past her. He went into the kitchen. The farmer was sitting by the fire. Pal was in his lap.

Reader 1 "Now I will show the farmer that I am a better dog than Pal!" said Donkey.

Reader 2 Donkey started to run in a circle. As he ran, he knocked over the kitchen table. CRASH went the table. Then, Donkey chased a little mouse that was near the fire. "EEK!" screamed the mouse. Donkey knocked over a stack of dishes. SMASH went the dishes.

Reader 1 Then, Donkey tried to bark. "HEE-HAW-WOOF!" barked Donkey.

Reader 1 "Now I will jump into the farmer's lap!" said Donkey happily. He started to jump.

Reader 2 "HELP!" yelled the farmer. "The donkey has gone crazy!"

Reader 2 The farmer's wife grabbed her broom. She waved the broom in front of the donkey. "Go away!" she yelled. "Go back outside!" She chased Donkey out of the house.

Reader 1 Donkey walked slowly back to the barn. He pushed open the door. He lay down on his soft bed of straw.

Reader 2 "Well?" asked Goat. "How did it go? Do you have a new job?"

Reader 1 Donkey ate some sweet grain. Then, he said, "I am not sure that being a dog is the right job for me. Maybe I had better keep being a donkey. At least I know how to do that!"

Name: _____

Donkey Changes Jobs: Checking for Details

Directions: Read each sentence about the story. Write a "**T**" on the blank if the sentence is true. Write an "**F**" on the blank if the sentence is false.

1. Donkey had jobs to do every day. _____

2. Pal liked to run in circles and chase rabbits. _____

3. Sometimes, Pal helped Donkey with his work. _____

4. The farmer's wife told Donkey to stay inside the house. _____

5. Donkey ate sweet grain and slept on a soft bed of straw. _____

Directions: Read the question. Write your answer in the bubble.

What do you think Donkey is thinking?

What do you think Donkey is thinking here?

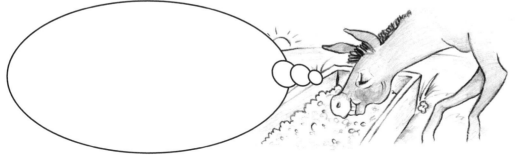

What do you think Donkey is thinking after all that had happened?

Name: _____

Donkey Changes Jobs: **Thinking About the Story**

Directions: Answer each question with a sentence.

1. What was Donkey's problem in the story?

_____

_____

_____

_____

_____

2. What lesson did Donkey learn?

_____

_____

3. How did Donkey feel about Pal at the end of the story? Explain.

_____

_____

_____

Try This! What things are you good at doing? Do people have to be good at doing everything? Write about your reasons on another sheet of paper.

– Teacher's Page –
Doctor Frog

Background
This story is based on the Aesop fable "The Quack Frog." One original moral for this story is "Physician, heal thyself." An easier moral to use for your students is "Deeds matter, not boasting."

Demonstrating Fluent Reading
Model fluent reading for your students by reading aloud the first page. After the reading, ask students to predict what might happen next in the story.

Select certain parts of the story and have different students take turns reading aloud those passages to the class. They can use the dialogue to make this more fun by adding a different emphasis to a line during each reading. For example, say, "Listen as I read this line: 'Sally said, We need a doctor.' Now listen as I read, 'We need a doctor?' and 'We need a doctor!' How is each one different?" Discuss as a class the meaning each emphasis adds.

Prereading Activity: Building Vocabulary
Before reading the story, review these vocabulary words with your students:

limped	thorn	ill	den
famous	secret	bottle	boasting

Reading with a Buddy
Pair students and have them be partners.

Day 1: Let students read aloud the story with "one voice" in unison to work on word recognition and fluency skills.

Day 2: Direct students to choose a part and read the story aloud again.

Day 3: Have students switch parts and reread the story to each other.

At the end of the third day, let your students show off how fluently they can read this story by taking home a copy of it. Encourage each student to read it aloud with a parent or another adult and then return the signed parent letter. (See page 6.)

Postreading Activities: Comprehension
Day 1: After they read the script aloud with partners, have the student pairs discuss what they liked about the story. Let them figure out the moral or lesson that the fable conveys.

Day 2: Have students work on the crossword puzzle activity to finish page 30.

Day 3: Direct students to complete the activity Thinking About the Story on page 31 by analyzing story elements and Doctor Frog's behavior and by identifying the lesson learned.

Character Education Connection
Discuss the moral of the story.
- Have you ever said you could do something, but you knew you could not?
- Why is it best not to brag?

Language Arts Connection
Read another book or story about boasting or bragging to the students. One possibility is the Zuni tale about a coyote bragging to the crows who teach him how to fly. Another is the pourquoi story, "How the Chipmunk Got His Stripes."

KE-804100 © Key Education　　　-27-　　　*Partner Read-Alouds: Aesop's Fables*

– The Fable –
Doctor Frog

Reader 1 "OW!" cried Sally Stork. "I hurt my bill on this stone."

Reader 2 Tricky Fox limped up to her. "I think I have a thorn in my paw," he said. "I was going to ask you to help me. Can you pull it out?"

Reader 1 "I cannot, now that my bill is hurt," said Sally.

Reader 2 Speedy Sparrow flew down from a tall tree. "Did you know that Will Wolf is not feeling well?" she said. "His nose is hot. That means he is ill."

Reader 1 Sally said, "We need a doctor."

Reader 2 "Yes!" said Tricky. "We need a doctor for all the animals in the woods."

Reader 1 "Speedy," said Sally, "you could go look for a doctor. You could fly over all of the woods. See if you can find somebody who can help us."

Reader 2 "I will!" said Speedy. She darted up into the sky.

Reader 1 The animals waited and waited. Sally's bill hurt so much she put her head under her wing. Tricky limped and hopped and complained.

Reader 2 Up in his den, Will Wolf woke up. He hurt all over. The wolf watched to see if the doctor had come yet.

Reader 1 "Look!" called Sally. "There is Speedy!"

Reader 2 "At last!" said Tricky.

Reader 1 Will Wolf slowly came out of his den and went down to hear what Speedy had to say.

Reader 2 "I found a doctor," said Speedy. "He is coming soon. It might take him a while. He has to hop the whole way."

Reader 1 "Hop? What kind of doctor is he?" asked Sally.

Reader 2 "His name is Doctor Frog," said Speedy.

Reader 1 "I have never heard of him," said Tricky.

Reader 2 "He says that he is known far and wide," said Speedy.

Reader 1 The animals waited. Then, they heard a voice.

Reader 2 "I am here!" said the voice. "I am the famous Doctor Frog!" A frog hopped out of the woods. He wore a black hat on his head, and he held a bottle.

Reader 1 "What is in that bottle?" asked Sally.

Reader 2 "This? This is a secret cure!" said Doctor Frog. "The cure in this bottle can help you if you feel bad."

Reader 1 "Can it take thorns out of paws?" asked Tricky.

Reader 2 "Of course!" said Doctor Frog.

Reader 1 "Can it help make Will Wolf feel better?" asked Speedy.

Reader 2 "Yes!" said Doctor Frog.

Reader 1 Sally looked at the bottle. "It looks like water from the pond," she said. Then, she looked closely at Doctor Frog. She asked, "Can you use this drink to make green skin turn pink?"

Reader 2 "Yes!" said Doctor Frog. "It can do anything!"

Reader 1 "Then, drink it," said Tricky. "Let's see if you turn into a pretty pink frog."

Reader 2 Doctor Frog blinked. "Umm . . . it might not work that fast," he said.

Reader 1 "Can you use this drink to fix eyes that stick out?" asked Sally.

Reader 2 "Of course!" said Doctor Frog. "My cures are famous!"

Reader 1 "Then drink it," said Tricky. "Let's see if it fixes your eyes."

Reader 2 Doctor Frog looked at the bottle. He looked at the animals. Then, he backed up slowly. "I will leave you this bottle," he said. "I must be on my way." He started to hurry off. When he was far away in the woods, he shouted to other animals, "Here I come! I am the famous Doctor Frog!"

Reader 1 Sally laughed. "Tricky, I think I can help you pull out that thorn now," she said. "Then, you can take some soup to Will Wolf. I don't think that silly boasting frog can help us. We will just have to help ourselves!"

Name: _____

Directions: Use the words in the Word Bank to complete the crossword puzzle.

Word Bank
boasting
bottle
doctor
famous
frog
paw
thorn
woods

Across

2. Doctor Frog showed the animals a _____.

5. Doctor Frog claimed his cures were _____.

7. Tricky needed a _____ pulled out of his paw.

8. The doctor was a _____.

Down

1. Sally knew the _____ frog couldn't help them.

3. Tricky had a _____ that hurt.

4. The animals in the _____ needed a doctor.

6. The frog claimed to be a _____.

Directions: Design a label for Doctor Frog's bottle.

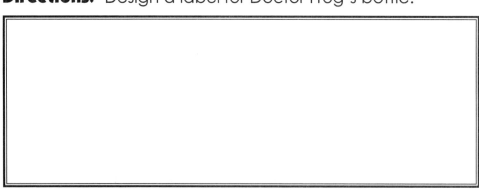

Name: _____

Doctor Frog: Thinking About the Story

Directions: Use the story. Fill in the chart.

1. Tell where the story takes place *(setting)* and the main characters.

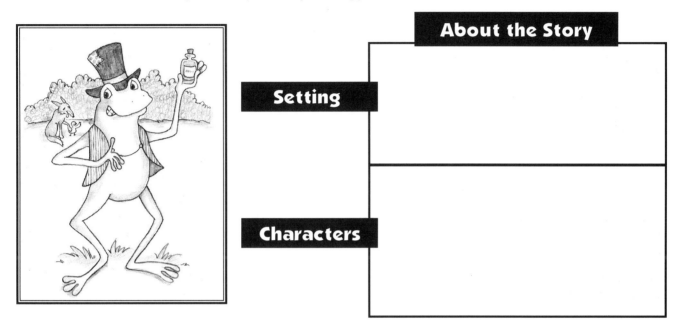

About the Story

Setting

Characters

Directions: Answer each question with a sentence.

2. Why did Doctor Frog want the animals to think he was famous?

_____

_____

3. What lesson did Sally and Tricky learn?

_____

_____

_____

Tell a Fable! Make up a story about an animal that must learn the lesson "Deeds matter, not boasting." Work with a partner and write the fable on paper.

– Teacher's Page –
A Guest for Dinner

Background

This story is based on the Aesop fable "The Fox and the Stork." There are several versions of the moral to this story, but one version could be summed up as "Treat your guests the way that you would like to be treated."

Demonstrating Fluent Reading

Model fluent reading for your students by reading aloud the first page. After the reading, ask students to predict what might happen next in the story.

Be sure to point out the impact of pauses. In this story, there are several places where dashes indicate a pause, such as, "And, she is making my favorite—fish soup!" Explain to your students that these dashes are just like drawing a breath before you finish the sentence. Read them with a dramatic flair to emphasize the pauses.

There are also many questions in this story. Show the students how a question requires that you inflect your voice at the end of the sentence. Have them ask you questions and listen to themselves as they speak. Then, repeat the question back to the students, using your hand to emphasize the lifting inflection.

Prereading Activity: Building Vocabulary

Before reading the story, review these vocabulary words with your students:

polite	foolish	trotted	favorite
stump	shallow	welcome	starving

Reading with a Buddy

Pair students and have them be partners.

Day 1: Let students read aloud the story with "one voice" in unison to work on word recognition and fluency skills.

Day 2: Direct students to choose a part and read the story aloud again.

Day 3: Have students switch parts and reread the story to each other.

At the end of the third day, let your students show off how fluently they can read this story by taking home a copy of it. Encourage each student to read it aloud with a parent or another adult and then return the signed parent letter. (See page 6.)

Postreading Activities: Comprehension

Day 1: After they read the script aloud with partners, have the student pairs discuss what they liked about the story. Let them figure out the moral or lesson that the fable conveys.

Day 2: Have students work on page 35, using the vocabulary to finish the sentences and then cutting out and sequencing the events.

Day 3: Direct students to complete the activity Thinking About the Story on page 36 by analyzing story elements and identifying lesson learned.

Character Education Connection

Discuss the moral of the story.
- Has someone ever done something special for you that made you feel comfortable? What was it?
- What would the two dinners in the story have been like if each animal was thinking about pleasing the other one when they set their tables?

Language Connection

Ask students to make up dialogue for Tricky and Sally as if they both were being good hosts to their guests. Students can try to write their words down after they brainstorm together.

– The Fable –

A Guest for Dinner

Reader 1 "Sally Stork thinks she is so great!" said Tricky Fox. He had just seen the huge bird flying across the sky. "She is so polite. She is so pretty. I wish that just once she would look silly and foolish!" Suddenly, Tricky had a plan.

Reader 1 Sally had a nest on top of an old barn. Tricky trotted over to the barn. He called, "Sally, are you home?'

Reader 2 "Hello, Tricky," said Sally from the top of the barn.

Reader 1 "I just caught some good fish," said Tricky. "I am making my favorite meal — fish soup! Would you like to come for dinner?"

Reader 2 "Why, Tricky! That is very nice. I would love to come," said Sally politely.

Reader 1 That night, Sally flew to Tricky's den. Outside, there was a tree stump. Tricky used it for a table. He had put two shallow bowls on the stump. "Here is our soup," said Tricky. "It's all ready! Please eat."

Reader 2 But, Sally had a problem. A stork has a long beak called a bill. Sally's bill was so long that she could not eat from the shallow little bowl. It was not deep enough.

Reader 1 Tricky lapped up all of his soup. He thought, "Sally looks so silly! She cannot eat her soup from that bowl! She looks funny. I am enjoying this."

Reader 1 Out loud, Tricky said, "Sally! I am sorry you do not like my soup."

Reader 2 "The soup is very good," said Sally politely.

Reader 1 "You don't seem to be eating much of it," said Tricky.

Reader 2 Sally thought, "That Tricky! He is full of tricks. But, I have a plan." Out loud, Sally said, "I think your fish soup is better than mine."

Reader 1 "Really?" said Tricky. "Thank you! But I am sure yours is good, too."

Reader 2 Sally said, "Would you like to try it? I am going fishing tomorrow. I will make fish soup. Then, you can come to dinner at my house."

Reader 1 "I would love to come to dinner," Tricky said.

Reader 1 The next day, Tricky looked everywhere for food. He could not find anything to eat.

Reader 1 "It's OK," said Tricky. "I am going to Sally's house for dinner. And, she is making my favorite — fish soup!"

Reader 2 That night, Tricky trotted over to the old barn. Sally was watching from the roof. "Welcome," she called. "Dinner is ready. Are you hungry?"

Reader 1 "I am starving!" said Tricky.

Reader 2 Sally had set up a table. On the table were two tall, thin vases. Steam rose out of them. "I hope you like my soup," she said. "I cooked all afternoon."

Reader 2 Sally leaned over one of the vases. She put her long, thin bill into the long, thin vase. She sipped some fish soup.

Reader 2 "I think it turned out well," she said. "What do you think, Tricky?"

Reader 1 Tricky sniffed around the top of the vase. "It smells good," he said. He tried to push his nose down into the vase so that he could get to the soup. His nose got stuck. He pulled his nose out — POP!

Reader 1 He licked a few drops from the top of the vase. "It tastes good, too," said the hungry fox.

Reader 2 Sally smiled again. "Good," she said. "I hope you enjoy it as much as I enjoyed your soup last night." Then, she put her long bill into her vase and ate all of her tasty fish soup.

Reader 1 Tricky went home just as hungry as he had been when he came to Sally's house. Maybe this time he was smarter, too.

Name: _____

Directions: Use the vocabulary to complete the sentences.

Vocabulary:	afternoon	barn	better	bowls
	dinner	fish	nose	plan	problem
	Sally	smelled	soup	trotted	vases

Tricky Fox wanted Sally Stork to look silly and foolish. So he made a _____.

One day, he trotted over to the old _____. He invited Sally to come for _____ at his den.

Tricky cooked _____ soup. He filled two shallow _____ and set them on a tree stump.

Sally joined Tricky for dinner. But, she had a _____. She couldn't sip the _____ from the bowl.

So she told Tricky that his soup was _____ than hers. Then, _____ invited him over for dinner.

The next day, Tricky _____ to Sally's house for dinner.

Sally had cooked all _____. She filled two, thin _____ with hot fish soup.

The soup _____ good. Tricky tried to stick his _____ into the vase, but couldn't. Sally ate all of her tasty soup.

Try This! Cut out the sentences. Mix them up. Then, paste them in order on a sheet of paper so that the story makes sense.

Name:

A Guest for Dinner: Thinking About the Story

Directions: Answer each question with a sentence.

1. Why did Tricky Fox make a plan in the story?

_____

_____

_____

2. What was Sally's problem in the story?

_____

_____

3. Do you think Tricky learned a lesson? Explain.

_____

_____

_____

4. What did you learn from the story?

_____

_____

Try This! On another paper, tell why it is important to make guests comfortable.

Jack and the Wolf

Background
This story is based on the Aesop fable "The House Dog and the Wolf." One moral for this story could be "To each his own."

Demonstrating Fluent Reading
Model fluent reading for your students by reading aloud the first page. After the reading, ask students to predict what might happen next in the story.

Be sure to highlight and discuss the treatment of a dialogue section. Use part of the talk between Jack and the wolf. Ask students, "Did you hear how I dropped my voice when the text read 'said the wolf'? I did this because that is not part of what they are saying out loud; it just tells us who is talking." Point out to your students that your voice is more expressive when you are reading the actual dialogue. Pair students and have them practice reading just the dialogue out loud.

Prereading Activity: Building Vocabulary
Before reading the story, review these vocabulary words with your students:

collar	crunched	guard	howl
sprang	wiggled	cousin	clinked

Reading with a Buddy
Pair students and have them be partners.

Day 1: Let students read aloud the story with "one voice" in unison to work on word recognition and fluency skills.

Day 2: Direct students to choose a part and read the story aloud again.

Day 3: Have students switch parts and reread the story to each other.

At the end of the third day, let your students show off how fluently they can read this story by taking home a copy of it. Encourage each student to read it aloud with a parent or another adult and then return the signed parent letter. (See page 6.)

Postreading Activities: Comprehension
Day 1: After they read the script aloud with partners, have the student pairs discuss what they liked about the story. Let them figure out the moral or lesson that the fable conveys.

Day 2: Have students work on page 40 by comparing and contrasting characters.

Day 3: Direct students to complete the activity Thinking About the Story on page 41 by analyzing story elements and identifying the lesson learned.

Character Education Connection
Discuss the moral of the story.
- Have you ever wished you could live somebody else's life?
- How do Jack and the wolf each feel at the end of the story? Why?

Arts Connection
Do a theatrical version of "Jack and the Wolf." In addition to the speaking parts, have students create sound effects. For example, one group of students can portray the wolf pack and howl in answer to Cousin Wolf! Perform your play for a younger group of students. Kindergartners would surely enjoy the performance.

– The Fable –
Jack and the Wolf

Reader 1 "You are a good dog, Jack," said Farmer Wellbeak. He patted Jack on the head. Then, he put the chain on Jack's collar. "I know you will watch our house tonight." The farmer walked away. His feet crunched in the snow.

Reader 2 Jack watched the farmer go inside. It was Jack's main job to guard the farmhouse at night. He had his own little house, filled with hay and blankets. He went inside and lay down. His nose faced out. That way he could watch for any trouble.

Reader 1 Jack heard a long howl. He lifted his head. Wolves! Jack heard them a lot. "Oh, how I wish I could run free with my cousins, the wolves!" thought Jack. "Night after night, I watch the house. I have this chain to keep me here. But, if the chain broke, I could live with the wolves!"

Reader 2 Jack thought about that. He would run anywhere he wanted. He would not have a job. He could do whatever he liked. He could howl all night long!

Reader 1 Instead, Jack watched the stone wall. He watched the fields. He watched the garden. Except for a few mice, he did not see anything. Jack sighed.

Reader 2 Suddenly, he heard a twig snap. Jack sprang to his feet! He ran to the end of his chain. His nose wiggled. A dark shape moved across the yard. It was a wolf!

Reader 1 "Don't bark, Cousin Dog," said the wolf. "I will not hurt you." The wolf limped up to Jack. They sniffed each other.

Reader 2 "Hello, Cousin Wolf," said Jack politely.

Reader 1 "Hello," said the wolf. "Do you . . . do you have anything that I could eat?

Reader 2 Jack looked at the wolf. He was very thin. He looked hungry. "Yes, I have this bone. It was part of my dinner. You can have it," said Jack.

Reader 1 He pushed the bone over to the wolf. The wolf fell on the bone. He chewed and chewed. When he was done, he said, "That was so good! Do you have food like that often?"

Reader 2 Jack was surprised. "Every night!" he said. "I always get a treat from dinner. But, I have my own food, too."

Reader 1 The wolf shook his head. "That is nice," he said. "Now, in the winter, we wolves are always hungry. There is so little food! Are you never hungry?"

Reader 2 "That's right," said Jack. "Farmer Wellbeak feeds me every day."

Reader 1 "What do you do for this food?" asked the wolf.

Reader 2 Jack said, "My job is to watch at night. I bark when I see strangers. I keep the house safe." His chain clinked. The wolf looked at it.

Reader 1 "What is that terrible thing?" he asked.

Reader 2 "This is my chain," said Jack. "It keeps me from running away."

Reader 1 The wolf backed up. "So, you cannot run free?" he asked. He sounded scared.

Reader 2 "No," said Jack.

Reader 1 The wolf shook his head. "I would rather be hungry! I could never wear a chain. I have to be free!" He ran across the field. Then, he turned and called, "I am sorry for you, Cousin!" Then, the wolf howled.

Reader 2 In the cold air the howl sounded very loud. Jack watched the wolf run until he was out of sight.

Reader 1 Jack lay back down on his warm blanket. He thought about his good meals. He thought about how he slept in the warm kitchen during the day so that he could be awake at night. He thought about Farmer Wellbeak.

Reader 2 "I thought I wanted to be free like the wolf," said Jack. "But, I am free in another way. I am never hungry. I have an important job to do. And, I am loved." Jack felt very happy. He was glad he had met his cousin, the wolf.

Name:

Jack and the Wolf:
Comparing and Contrasting Characters

Directions: Read the words in the boxes below. Which words tell about Jack?
Which words tell about the wolf? Which words tell about both animals?
Cut out the words. Glue each one in the correct section of the Venn diagram.

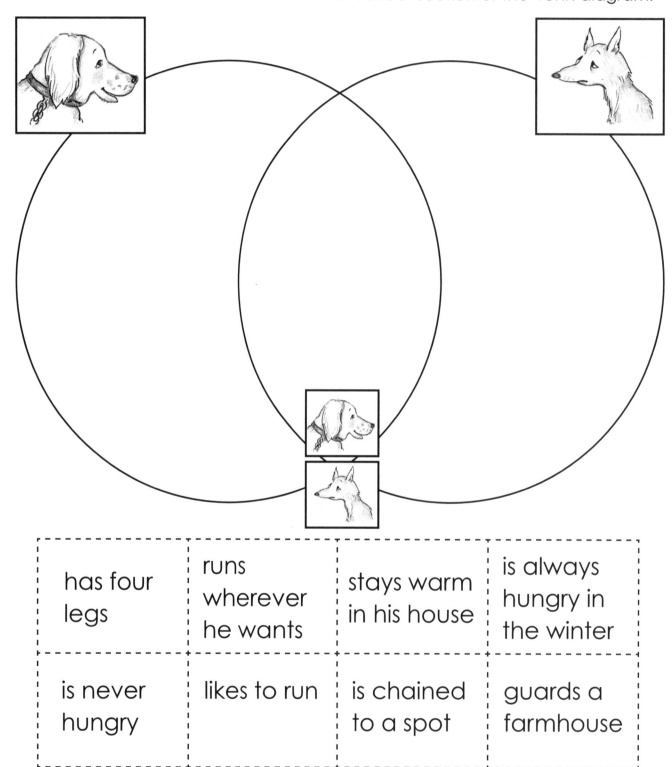

has four legs	runs wherever he wants	stays warm in his house	is always hungry in the winter
is never hungry	likes to run	is chained to a spot	guards a farmhouse

Name: _____

Jack and the Wolf: Thinking About the Story

Directions: Use the story. Fill in the chart.

1. Tell where the story takes place *(setting)* and the main characters.

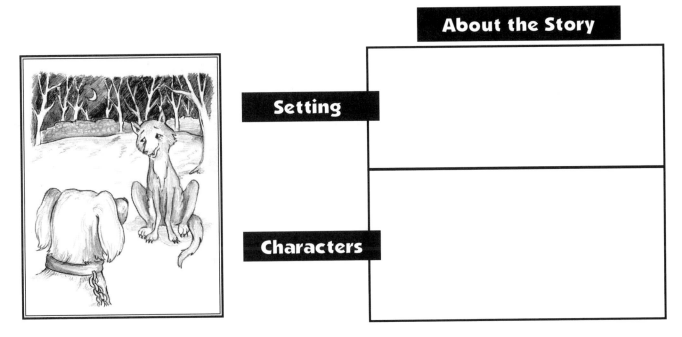

About the Story

Setting	
Characters	

Directions: Answer each question with a sentence.

2. What was Jack's problem in the story?

_____

_____

3. What lesson did Jack learn?

_____

_____

Try This! What are the best parts of your own life? Explain your answer on a sheet of paper.

– Teacher's Page –
Betsy and Bossy

Background
This story is based on the Aesop fable "The Milkmaid and Her Pail." The original moral of this story is what Greta Goat observes: "Don't count your chickens before they're hatched."

Day 1: Let students read aloud the story with "one voice" in unison to work on word recognition and fluency skills.

Day 2: Direct students to choose a part and read the story aloud again.

Day 3: Have students switch parts and reread the story to each other.

At the end of the third day, let your students show off how fluently they can read this story by taking home a copy of it. Encourage each student to read it aloud with a parent or another adult and then return the signed parent letter. (See page 6.)

Postreading Activities: Comprehension
Day 1: After they read the script aloud with partners, have the student pairs discuss what they liked about the story. Let them figure out the moral or lesson that the fable conveys.

Day 2: Have students work on page 45 by recalling details and applying creative ideas.

Day 3: Direct students to complete the activity Thinking About the Story on page 46 by analyzing Betsy's actions, making an inference, and identifying the lesson learned.

Demonstrating Fluent Reading
Model fluent reading for your students by reading aloud the first page. After the reading, ask students to predict what might happen next in the story.

Be sure to draw attention to the challenging dialogue section. Model and discuss how you handled the lines where Bossy "talks" to Betsy through physical actions. The line, "That meant . . . " appears, followed by Bossy's reply in human language. Point out that the phrase "that meant" in these sentences is used very much like the word "said" in regular dialogue. Show students how you pause after "that meant" in the same way as pausing after the word "said."

Character Education Connection
Discuss the moral of the story.
- Have you ever counted on something happening and then it didn't? How did you feel?
- What can happen when you "count your chickens before they're hatched"?
- Is it better to want something you don't have, or to like what you do have?

Prereading Activity: Building Vocabulary
Before reading the story, review these vocabulary words with your students:

sighed	milked	stool	hatch
rich	trade	toss	spilled

Math Connection
Invite students to generate "chickens before they're hatched" story problems! Have them work with partners and write down the problems on paper for classmates to solve. Here is an example: "If you could get two dollars for your butter and the eggs are ten cents each, how many eggs could you buy?"

Reading with a Buddy
Pair students and have them be partners.

Reader 1 "Milking time, Bossy!" called Betsy. Bossy sighed. She did not mind being milked. But, Betsy talked and talked and talked. Bossy liked her barn. The sun came in through the windows. The hay was sweet and tasty. And, it was nice and quiet— except at milking time.

Reader 2 "Good afternoon, Bossy!" said Betsy. She was carrying her pail on her head. Betsy liked to carry the pail this way. "I hope you had a good day." Bossy swished her tail. That meant, "Yes."

Reader 1 "That's great!" said Betsy. "Guess where I am going tonight? I'm going to the dance. All the farmers will be there. Farmer Jones will be there. And, I bet his son Jeff will be there, too. Jeff thinks he is so wonderful," said Betsy. She set down the pail. She got the stool to sit on. "Just because he is good-looking! Well, I would never marry him!"

Reader 2 Bossy listened quietly. She knew that Betsy liked Jeff the best.

Reader 1 "I wish I had a new dress to wear," said Betsy as she started to milk the cow. "I would like a pink dress. Or, maybe a blue one . . . something with a nice, big bow in the back. What do you think?"

Reader 2 Bossy gave a low moo. That meant, "It sounds nice."

Reader 1 "I think it would be pretty, too! Mother says we do not have enough money to buy a new dress right now. But, who knows? Maybe we will have a good year. We might plant some extra wheat. Then, we will have more to sell when we cut it. Or, maybe we could buy some eggs."

Reader 2 Bossy stamped her foot. That meant, "Why do you want eggs?"

Reader 1 "Oh, Bossy! Everybody knows that. You get the eggs to hatch. Then, you have little chicks. They grow up to be hens. They lay more eggs. Then, you can sell some eggs and hatch some so that you have more chickens."

Reader 2 Bossy nodded her head. That meant, "I see."

Reader 1 "Look at this good, rich milk you just gave me, Bossy!" said Betsy. She stood up with the milking pail. "I know what I will do. I will make butter with this milk. Then, I will take the butter into town. I will trade it for some eggs. Then, I will raise some little chicks. Soon I'll have eggs to sell!"

Reader 2 Bossy listened. Betsy lifted the pail and put it on her head.

Reader 1 "When I sell my eggs, I will have money for my new pink dress! Or, maybe it will be a blue one. Then, I can wear the dress at the next dance! All of the boys will come and ask me to dance. But, if that Jeff Jones comes to ask me . . . Why do you know what I will do?"

Reader 2 Bossy shook her head. That meant, "No, I don't know."

Reader 1 "Why, Bossy, I would never dance with that stuck-up Jeff! I won't even say no to him. I'll just toss my head — like this!"

Reader 2 Bossy raised her head and flicked her ears. That meant, "Watch out!" But, it was too late. When Betsy tossed her head, the pail fell off and crashed on the ground. All of the milk ran out across the floor of the barn.

Reader 1 "Oh, no! My butter! My eggs! My chicks! My new dress!" cried Betsy. Then, she ran from the barn.

Reader 2 Bossy looked at the spilled milk. She gave a low moo.

Reader 1 Greta Goat looked over from her end of the barn. "That Betsy is a silly girl," said Greta.

Reader 2 "She does talk a lot," said Bossy. "And, she dreams a lot, too."

Reader 1 "Well," said Greta, "I think it is smart not to count your chickens before they hatch!"

Name: _____

Betsy and Bossy: Checking for Details

Directions: Read each sentence about the story. Write a "**T**" on the blank if the sentence is true. Write an "**F**" on the blank if the sentence is false.

1. Betsy liked to carry the milk pail on her head. _____

2. Betsy wished for a new dress to wear to the dance. _____

3. Betsy planned to sell Bossy's milk. _____

4. She hoped to raise chickens so that she could sell eggs to earn money. _____

5. The milk was spilled on the floor in Betsy's house. _____

6. Betsy bought a new dress with a big bow in the back. _____

Directions: What other things could Betsy do to earn money for a new dress? Make a list. To get started, you may include some ideas from the story.

Betsy and Bossy: Thinking About the Story

Directions: Use words from the story to fill in the boxes.

1. Betsy told Bossy her plans for making money. What were her plans?

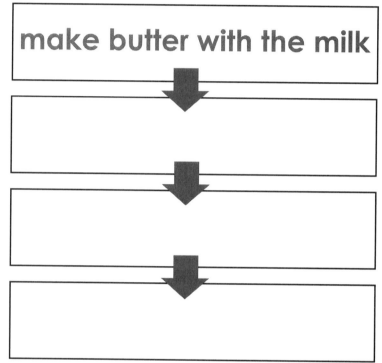

make butter with the milk

Directions: Answer each question with a sentence.

2. How did Betsy feel when she spilled the milk on the floor? Explain.

_____

_____

_____

3. What lesson did you learn from this story?

_____

_____

Tell a Fable! Write a different story using animals that teaches the same lesson.

The Dog and His Treat

Background

This story is based on the Aesop fable "The Dog and the Bone." There are several versions of the moral to this story, but one version is "Only a fool is greedy."

Demonstrating Fluent Reading

Model fluent reading for your students by reading aloud the first page. After the reading, ask students to predict what might happen next in the story.

Be to sure model and discuss how you handled the section where the farm animals are calling out to Rufus. Point out that the author has incorporated animal sounds in some of the words. Say, "Why do the geese say, 'Rufusssss' instead of 'Rufus'? What sound do geese make?" Exaggerate each animal sound and then encourage students to mimic your readings as they follow along in the text.

Prereading Activity: Building Vocabulary

Before reading the story, review these vocabulary words with your students:

treat	perfect	juicy	drooled
honked	hissed	pasture	nerve

Draw attention to the idiom in the story: " 'Of all the nerve!' thought Rufus."

Reading with a Buddy

Pair students and have them be partners.

Day 1: Let students read aloud the story with "one voice" in unison to work on word recognition and fluency skills.

Day 2: Direct students to choose a part and read the story aloud again.

Day 3: Have students switch parts and reread the story to each other.

At the end of the third day, let your students show off how fluently they can read this story by taking home a copy of it. Encourage each student to read it aloud with a parent or another adult and then return the signed parent letter. (See page 6.)

Postreading Activities: Comprehension

Day 1: After they read the script aloud with partners, have the student pairs discuss what they liked about the story. Let them figure out the moral or lesson that the fable conveys.

Day 2: Have students work on page 50 by using vocabulary to finish the sentences and by sequencing events.

Day 3: Direct students to complete the activity Thinking About the Story on page 51 by analyzing the Rufus's traits and actions and identifying the lesson learned.

Character Education Connection

Discuss the moral of the story.

- Have you ever wanted something that someone else had?
- Why do you think it might be better to be happy with what you have instead?
- What happened to Rufus because he was greedy?

Social Studies Connection

Talk about a farm as a community of animals. Which animals get along? Which animals do not? What role does each animal have in the community?

The Dog and His Treat

Reader 1 "There you go, Rufus!" said kind Farmer Jones. He set down something in front of Rufus. He patted the dog on the head. "I wanted to give you a big treat because you have been such a good dog. Enjoy it!"

Reader 2 Rufus looked down at the bone. It was perfect. It was juicy. It had big chunks of meat on it. Rufus drooled. "I will spend all afternoon enjoying my treat," he said to himself. "And, I will take my treat to my favorite place before I eat it!"

Reader 1 The dog picked up the bone and trotted off. There was a nice, cool place by the river that he liked. When he went there, he could sit in the shade. He barked at the birds. He drank nice, cold water from the river. And today, he would have a big, tasty bone to eat!

Reader 2 Rufus headed to the gate. A few geese honked at him and then hissed at him. They did not like Rufus. He barked at them. He chased them for fun. Sometimes, he ate their food! "Going ssssomewhere, Rufusssss?" one goose hissed.

Reader 1 Rufus nodded. He could not answer because he was carrying his treat in his mouth.

Reader 2 The dog trotted out into the pasture. One cow kicked her back legs when she saw the dog. The cows did not like Rufus either. Sometimes, he nipped their heels to get them to walk to the barn. "Moooove on, bad dog!" said the cow. The dog just walked past, carrying his treat.

Reader 1 Next, he trotted past the sheep. They ran up a hill to get as far away from Rufus as they could. Of all the farm animals, they liked Rufus the least. It was his job to herd them from one place to another. He barked at them. He bit them. Sometimes, he took their grain to eat! "Don't come baaaaack any time soon!" called one sheep.

Reader 2 Rufus pretended not to hear. He was used to animals that did not like him. "I have my treat. I am going to chew all afternoon," the dog thought to himself. He was happy. He loved treats. He loved food of any kind.

Reader 1 Rufus had to cross a little bridge to get to his favorite place. As he was trotting across, he looked down at the water. There was another dog! "Hey!" thought Rufus. "That dog should not be here." Rufus growled at the dog in the water. The dog growled, too.

Reader 2 "Of all the nerve!" thought Rufus. Then, he looked closer. "Hey!" thought Rufus. "That dog has a bone, too. But look! His bone is bigger. It has more meat on it. It is better than mine!" Rufus was mad now. He growled again. The other silly dog growled, too.

Reader 1 Rufus did not think very well when he was mad. And, he was very mad. This dog was on his land! This dog would not run away! And, this dog had a better treat! "I'll show him," thought Rufus.

Reader 2 "I will bark and chase him. That will make him drop his bone. Then, I will have two treats to eat this afternoon!" Rufus drooled at the thought of two treats instead of one.

Reader 1 Rufus barked. The bone fell out of his mouth. It landed in the river with a big SPLASH. Rufus dove at the other dog. He landed in the river with a big SPLASH. But, once he was in the water, the other dog was gone! Rufus did not know it, but he had been looking at himself.

Reader 2 "That dog took my treat!" said Rufus. "My treat is gone. How I wish I had held onto it!" Sadly, the dog climbed out of the river. He sat on a big stone. He thought about his lost bone. "Next time," the dog told himself, "I will enjoy my own treat. I won't worry about always having more."

Name: _____

Directions: Use the vocabulary to complete the sentences.

Vocabulary:	barked	bigger	bone	bridge
dog	dove	geese	mouth	pasture
pretended	river	Rufus	sheep	treat

One day, Farmer Jones gave _____ a big treat.

Rufus picked up the _____. He trotted off to the _____.

The _____ passed through the gate. One of the _____ hissed at him.

Next, Rufus walked past a cow in the _____ . The cow called him a "bad dog."

Then, the dog passed a flock of _____ . Rufus _____ not to hear the mean words the sheep said.

Finally, Rufus reached the _____ over the river. He started across. He saw another dog in the water. That dog had a bigger _____!

Rufus was very mad. He _____ at the other dog. The bone fell out of his _____. It hit the water with a big SPLASH!

Rufus wanted that _____ bone. He _____ at the other dog and into the water. But, the other dog was gone!

Try This! Cut out the sentences. Mix them up. Then, paste them in order on a sheet of paper so that the story makes sense.

Analyzing, Drawing Conclusions

The Dog and His Treat: Thinking About the Story

Directions: Answer each question with a sentence.

1. How would you describe Rufus and his actions at the beginning of the story?

_____

_____

_____

_____

2. What do you think made Rufus maddest when he saw the other dog?

_____

_____

_____

3. What did you learn from the story?

_____

_____

_____

Tell a Fable! Plan a different story about a greedy animal that learns an important lesson. Write your fable on a sheet of paper.

A Friend Indeed

Background
This story is based on the Aesop fable "The Ant and the Dove." The original moral of this story is "One good turn deserves another."

Demonstrating Fluent Reading
Model fluent reading for your students by reading aloud the first page. After the reading, ask students to predict what might happen next in the story.

Be sure to model and discuss your treatment of a rhyming section. Use Andy's poem from the end of the story. Tell students, "Listen again to how I grouped the words 'Hooray for the dove!' I did this because it is a whole thought that belongs together. Then, I paused before I read, 'Out of kindness and love'." Point out to students how your voice sounded louder when you read, "Hooray for the dove!" Explain that you did this to show Andy was cheering for his new friend.

To extend fluency practice, write Andy's poem on the board. Then, have students do a choral reading. The poem's rhythm is an effective tool for helping students practice clustering words in meaningful groups.

Prereading Activity: Building Vocabulary
Before reading the story, review these vocabulary words with your students:

wow	break	dodged	breeze	bank
slope	clung	peck	jaws	swat

Reading with a Buddy
Pair students and have them be partners.

Day 1: Let students read aloud the story with "one voice" in unison to work on word recognition and fluency skills.

Day 2: Direct students to choose a part and read the story aloud again.

Day 3: Have students switch parts and reread the story to each other.

At the end of the third day, let your students show off how fluently they can read this story by taking home a copy of it. Encourage each student to read it aloud with a parent or another adult and then return the signed parent letter. (See page 6.)

Postreading Activities: Comprehension
Day 1: After they read the script aloud with partners, have the student pairs discuss what they liked about the story. Let them figure out the moral or lesson that the fable conveys.

Day 2: Have students work on page 55 by identifying cause and effect and by making an inference.

Day 3: Direct students to complete the activity Thinking About the Story on page 56 by analyzing story elements and Andy's actions and by identifying the lesson learned.

Character Education Connection
Discuss the moral of the story.
- Name something nice you have done for a friend.
- Do you think that when you do something nice for somebody that they would like to do something nice for you in return? Why or why not?
- How does it feel when you help somebody else?

Thinking Skills Connection
Ask students, "How big is an ant?" Have them draw a life-sized picture. View photos of ants in books to learn about their features and find out more about different kinds of ants. Then, brainstorm how the world might be for an ant. If a leaf is big enough to be a boat, what could an ant use as a table? A chair? A house?

A Friend Indeed

Reader 1 One bright spring day, Andy Ant headed for the pond. He had been working hard on a new nest. He had pushed sand and pulled out tiny stones. He had dug dirt. "Wow!" said Andy. "I am tired. I am thirsty, too! I need a rest. A nice, cold drink of water would make a good break."

Reader 2 Andy walked to the pond. It had rained the night before. Andy had to scoot out of the way as drops of water came down from the leaves. "Watch out!" he told himself as he dodged a big drop. "Look out!" he cried as the breeze shook a branch, and water rained down from it. Andy was so small that he could drown in a drop of water. He had to be very careful.

Reader 1 Andy was still running from all of the water when he got to the pond. And then, suddenly, Andy could not stop.

Reader 2 The bank of the small pond was muddy and wet. Andy's thin little legs slipped out to the right and to the left. He slid down the slope to the water. Then, he slid right in!

Reader 1 "Oh, no!" cried Andy. He tried to swim. He waved his thin little legs. "Help, somebody!"

Reader 2 Just as Andy was starting to slip under the water, he saw a pair of big, light gray wings over him. A voice said, "Here's a leaf. Climb on!" Andy saw the green edge of a leaf on the water. He clung to it. He pulled himself on board. The leaf was just like a boat for the little ant.

Reader 1 On the shore, he saw a beautiful dove. She was watching as he floated on his green-leaf boat.

Reader 2 "I saw you in the water," she said softly. "I pulled that leaf off a tree. I threw it into the water for you."

Reader 1 "Thank you!" said Andy. "That was very kind of you." His leaf boat started to float to the shore.

Reader 2 "You are welcome," said the dove. She started to peck at seeds that had fallen off a tree in the rain.

Reader 1 Andy's leaf arrived at the shore. Carefully, he stepped onto the muddy bank. Then, slowly he started to climb up the slope. As he did, he saw something move in the bushes.

Reader 2 Andy looked harder. It was a hunter! The hunter was dressed in black clothes. He was hidden behind the leaves. He was looking at the dove. In his hand he held a net.

Reader 1 "He is going to try to catch my new friend!" thought Andy. "He will catch her and eat her. What can I do?"

Reader 2 He did not stop to think. Instead, the brave little ant ran up the muddy slope. He raced into the bushes. He found the foot of the hunter. He opened his jaws. Then, he bit the hunter as hard as he could.

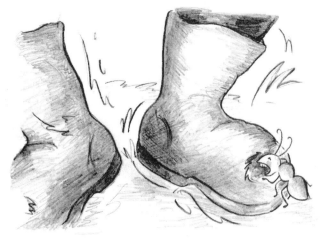

Reader 1 "Ouch!" cried the hunter. Before the hunter could lean down to swat him, Andy ran under a leaf to hide. He looked up. The dove had heard and seen the hunter. She flew high up into a pine tree. The hunter could not reach there with his net. She was safe.

Reader 2 Andy headed home. He felt so good that he made up a poem about his day.

Reader 1 "Hooray for the dove!
Out of kindness and love,
She saved an ant,
Who hid in a plant
And saved her right back
From a hunter in black!"

Reader 2 Andy walked home. He scooted this way and that way to keep away from the drops of water. "I may be small enough to drown in a drop," Andy said out loud, "but I feel 10 feet tall!"

A Friend Indeed: Checking for Details

Directions: A **cause** makes something happen. An **effect** happens as a result of a cause. Write the cause or effect in the blank.

Cause		**Effect**

1. The bank of the pond was muddy and wet.

2. The dove dropped a leaf into the water.

3. _____

 The dove flew up into the tree for safety.

4. _____

 Andy had to scoot this way and that way when walking.

Directions: Read the question. Write your answer in the bubble.

What do you think Andy Ant is thinking when he first sees the dove?

Name: _____

A Friend Indeed: Thinking About the Story

Directions: Fill in the chart.

1. Tell where the story takes place *(setting)* and the main characters.

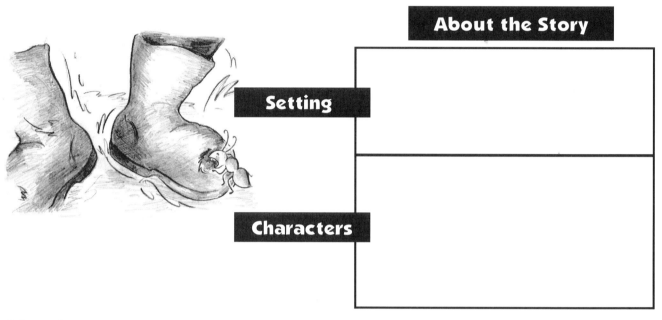

About the Story	
Setting	
Characters	

Directions: Answer each question with a sentence.

2. What was Andy Ant's problem with the hunter in the story?

_____

_____

3. What lesson did Andy learn?

_____

_____

_____

Try This! Think about a time when you did a good deed for someone in return for something that person did for you. Write about it on a sheet of paper.

Background
This story is based on the Aesop fable "The Fox and the Lion." The original moral of this story is "Familiarity breeds contempt."

Demonstrating Fluent Reading
Model fluent reading for your students by reading aloud the first page. After the reading, ask students to predict what might happen next in the story.

Be sure to demonstrate how an exclamation point is given the most emphasis of all marks. Tell students, "Listen to how I read the two lines, 'He looked at me. I think he was going to eat me!' I showed that emotion in my voice because Tricky was more scared of the idea of being eaten than he was when the lion just looked at him."

Point out to your students that you used a louder voice when you read, ". . . going to eat me!" Explain that this is how you could show that Tricky was truly scared of King Lion.

Another section to highlight for fluency practice is Tricky's song. During guided reading time, let students sing the song to the tune of "Frère Jacques." The song's rhythm will help students group the words correctly. After they have sung the text, have students read it in unison and listen for how they cluster the words into meaningful chunks.

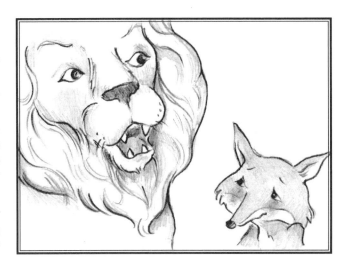

Prereading Activity: Building Vocabulary
Before reading the story, review these vocabulary words with your students:

fine	beat	dare	dove
fellow	berries	hurrying	roared

Reading with a Buddy
Pair students and have them be partners.

Day 1: Let students read aloud the story with "one voice" in unison to work on word recognition and fluency skills.

Day 2: Direct students to choose a part and read the story aloud again.

Day 3: Have students switch parts and reread the story to each other.

At the end of the third day, let your students show off how fluently they can read this story by taking home a copy of it. Encourage each student to read it aloud with a parent or another adult and then return the signed parent letter. (See page 6.)

Postreading Activities: Comprehension
Day 1: After they read the script aloud with partners, have the student pairs discuss what they liked about the story. Let them figure out the moral or lesson that the fable conveys.

Day 2: Have students work on page 60 by recalling story elements and details.

Day 3: Direct students to complete the activity Thinking About the Story on page 61 by analyzing the Tricky's traits and actions and identifying the lesson learned.

Character Education Connection
Discuss the moral of the story.
- Do you have a busy street near your house? Even though it is close to home, do you still have to stop and watch for traffic?
- Even if you see the same wild animal every day, might it still bite you?
- Are you as polite to people in your family as you are to strangers?

Science Connection
Aesop was a keen observer of animal behavior. He knew that a weaker animal would show submissiveness to a stronger one. Find examples of this behavior, such as when a small animal will roll up in a ball and not look directly at a bigger one. Talk about how this "respectful" behavior helps animals to survive.

– The Fable –
King Lion

Reader 1 Tricky Fox looked at himself in the pond. "What a fine animal I am!" said Tricky. "All of the other animals fear me. They know that I am tricky and smart. Nobody is better than me!" He smiled at his own face. Then, he started down the path in the woods, singing a loud song.

Reader 2 "Of all the animals that you see, I know that you'll agree, I am just the best— better than the rest! I love me! I love me!"

Reader 1 Suddenly, Tricky stopped. His heart started to beat very fast. A huge animal was standing in the path. He looked at Tricky. Then, he opened his mouth to yawn. Tricky saw rows of big, sharp teeth.

Reader 2 "Yip! Yip! Yip!" cried Tricky. He ran off the path and into the woods. He ran as fast as he could. He did not dare look back.

Reader 1 "Tricky, why are you running?" somebody called from a tree. It was Speedy Sparrow.

Reader 2 "I just saw the biggest animal I have ever seen," Tricky said, panting. "He looked at me. I think he was going to eat me!"

Reader 1 "That must have been King Lion," said Speedy. "I heard he was walking through our woods. He is the king of all the animals. Even you, Tricky!"

Reader 2 Tricky nodded. He was still shaking. The huge lion had scared him.

Reader 1 A few days later, Tricky was walking through the woods again. He looked up ahead. There was King Lion! Tricky dove into the bushes. He hid there. King Lion walked past. "He did not see me," said Tricky to himself. "But, maybe it wouldn't have been so bad if he had."

Reader 2 The next time Tricky saw King Lion, he did not hide. Instead, he stood at the side of the path. He bowed low. "Good day, King Lion," he said. "It's a fine day." The lion nodded and walked past.

Reader 1 Later that day, Tricky saw Greta Goat. "Where have you been, Tricky?" she asked.

Reader 2 "I was just talking with my friend, the king," bragged Tricky. "We were talking about the nice weather. King Lion said, 'Tricky, you know more about the weather than any other animal in the woods.'"

Reader 1 "King Lion said that?" asked Greta.

Reader 2 "That's right," said Tricky. "We are good friends."

Reader 1 A little later, Tricky saw Speedy Sparrow. "That King Lion is a fine fellow. He and I were just talking," Tricky told the little bird. "He is not scary at all."

Reader 2 "Really, Tricky?" asked Speedy.

Reader 1 "I should know," bragged Tricky. "We are best friends."

Reader 2 Each time Tricky saw King Lion in the woods, he would speak. The huge lion would nod and walk past.

Reader 1 "Why, I don't think he's a king at all," Tricky said to himself. "I should not fear him! He may be big, but he will not eat ME. After all, nobody is better than me!"

Reader 2 A few days later, Tricky went to pick some berries. He was hurrying down the path when he saw King Lion up ahead. "Hello there!" called Tricky. "Step aside, please. You are taking up the whole path. I am doing something very important."

Reader 1 King Lion looked at the fox. He opened his mouth. Then, he roared. The bushes shook. The trees moved back and forth. Tricky ran for dear life.

Reader 2 From that day on, Tricky always bowed or hid when King Lion walked by.

King Lion: Checking for Details

Directions: Read each clue. Use the story. Write the name of the character in the blanks. Match the name with the correct illustration.

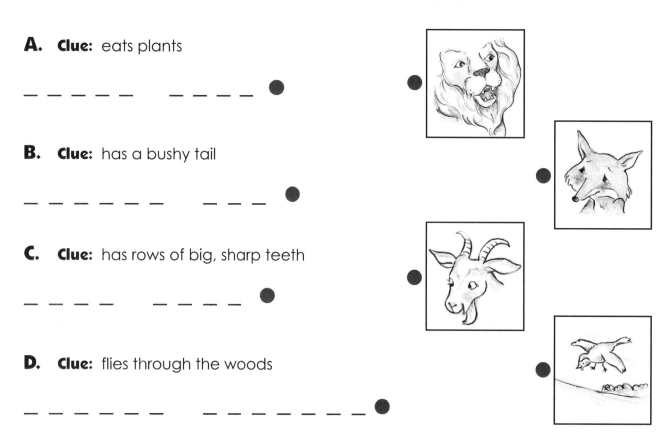

A. Clue: eats plants

_ _ _ _ _   _ _ _ _ •

B. Clue: has a bushy tail

_ _ _ _ _ _   _ _ _ •

C. Clue: has rows of big, sharp teeth

_ _ _ _   _ _ _ _ •

D. Clue: flies through the woods

_ _ _ _ _ _   _ _ _ _ _ _ •

Directions: Read each sentence about the story. Write a "**T**" on the blank if the sentence is true. Write an "**F**" on the blank if the sentence is false.

1. Greta Goat sings a song about herself.   _____

2. At first, Tricky thought the lion would eat him.   _____

3. Tricky told Greta that King Lion was his friend.   _____

4. Speedy agreed that King Lion was not scary.   _____

5. The bushes shook when King Lion roared.   _____

Name: _____

King Lion: Thinking About the Story

Directions: Answer each question with a sentence.

1. Use some words from the story to tell what Tricky Fox said.

What did Tricky tell Greta about his conversation with King Lion?

How did Tricky describe King Lion when talking to Speedy?

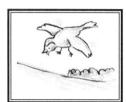

_____

_____

_____

_____

_____

_____

_____

_____

2. Describe Tricky's character traits in the story.

_____

_____

3. What lesson did Tricky learn?

_____

_____

_____

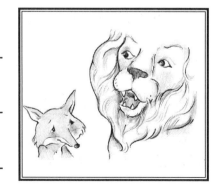

Tell a Fable! Plan a different story about animals to teach the lesson of showing respect to another creature. Write your story on a sheet of paper.

Answer Key

A Well of Trouble 10
Cause and Effect
1 a. Tricky wanted a drink and leaned too far into the well.
2 b. Greta took a long drink but then realized that she couldn't get out of the well.
3 a. Tricky jumped on Greta's back and scrambled up her long horns.
4 b. The farmer found Greta, and he and his helpers lifted her out of the well.

Bottom section
Answers will vary but may include: shady, dim, gloomy, shadowy, dusky, chilly, cold, nippy, clammy.

A Well of Trouble 11
1. Tricky Fox was untrustworthy, tricky, scheming, and clever.
   Greta Goat was silly, trusting, innocent, and teachable.
2. Greta could trust the farmer. As soon as he found Greta, he ran to get help and lifted her out of the well.
3. Greta learned to never trust the fox. She also learned that she should look before she leaps (to think carefully before doing something).

A Big Wish 15
1. sparrow, woods, 2. pond, 3. mirror, 4. ugly,
5. peacock, 6. feathers, 7. wings, 8. wished, self

Bottom section
Sparrow: Colors—gray, brown; Tail—short; Wings—small;
Peacock: Colors—blue, green; Tail—long feathers, opened like a fan, too heavy to fly; Wings—too heavy to fly

A Big Wish 15
Top section
Answers will vary.

1. Sidney saw himself in the pond and thought he was ugly.
2. Sidney was a beautiful peacock but could no longer fly or do the things he loved.
3. Sidney learned to be happy just the way he was.

The Great Peace 20
Top section
Answers will vary.

Word Find

```
l  a (h  o  n  e  s  t)
y  (f  r  i  e  n  d) f
i  p  s  l  y  o  p  e
n  r  u (h  e  n  s) a
g (a  n  i  m  a  l) s
(r  o  o  s  t  e  r) t
(b  r  o  t  h  e  r  s)
```

The Great Peace 21
1. Tricky Fox: careful, a planner, a thinker, a liar, untruthful; The rooster: careful, smart, clever
2. In the Great Peace, all animals would be friends. Tricky Fox made it up to try to trick the rooster to come closer so that Tricky could catch him.
3. Answers will vary. Liars get caught in their own lies.

Donkey Changes Jobs 25
1. T, 2. T, 3. F, 4. F, 5. T

Bottom section
Answers will vary.

Donkey Changes Jobs 26
1. Donkey wanted a new job because he worked all day long.
2. Donkey learned that he should be happy with who he was and satisfied with doing the job he knew how to do.
3. Answers will vary. Donkey was probably less envious when he realized that Pal was well suited to the job of being a dog just as he was good at the job of being a donkey.

Doctor Frog 30
Across: 2. bottle, 5. famous, 7. thorn, 8. frog

Down: 1. boasting, 3. paw, 4. woods, 6. doctor

Doctor Frog 30
1. Setting: woods; Characters: Sally Stork, Tricky Fox, Speedy Sparrow, Will Wolf, Doctor Frog
2. Doctor Frog wanted the animals to admire him and believe he was a well-known doctor who could cure any ailment.
3. Sally and Tricky learned not to believe someone's boastful words unless the promises were backed up with actions.

A Guest for Dinner 35
Tricky Fox wanted Sally Stork to look silly and foolish. So he made a <u>plan</u>. One day, he trotted over to the old <u>barn</u>. He invited Sally to come for <u>dinner</u> at his den. Tricky cooked <u>fish</u> soup. He filled two shallow <u>bowls</u> and set them on a tree stump. Sally joined Tricky for dinner. But, she had a <u>problem</u>. She couldn't sip the <u>soup</u> from the bowl. So she told Tricky that his soup was <u>better</u> than hers. Then, <u>Sally</u> invited him over for dinner. The next day, Tricky <u>trotted</u> to Sally's house for dinner. Sally had cooked all <u>afternoon</u>. She filed two, thin <u>vases</u> with hot fish soup. The soup <u>smelled</u> good. Tricky tried to stick his <u>nose</u> into the vase, but couldn't. Sally ate all of her tasty soup.

A Guest for Dinner 35
1. Tricky Fox wanted to make Sally Stork look silly and foolish.
2. Because Sally had a long bill, she could not eat Tricky's soup from a shallow bowl.
3. Answers will vary.
4. Answers will vary. Treat others the way you would like to be treated.

Jack and the Wolf 40
Jack: stays warm in his house, is never hungry, is chained to a spot, guards a farmhouse
Cousin Wolf: runs wherever he wants, is always hungry in the winter
Both: has four legs, likes to run

Jack and the Wolf 41
1. Setting: Farmer Wellbeak's farm; Characters: Farmer Wellbeak, Jack, Cousin Wolf
2. Jack wished to run free with his wolf cousins instead of being chained to his house.
3. Answers will vary. Jack learned that he was free to appreciate the good things he had, like plenty of food, a warm house, an important job, and love.

Betsy and Bossy 45
1. T, 2. T, 3. F, 4. T, 5. F, 6. F

Bottom section
Answers will vary.

Betsy and Bossy 46
1. make butter with the milk (given), trade butter for eggs, raise chicks, sell eggs
2. Betsy was upset that all of her plans to make money were ruined when she spilled the milk.
3. Answers will vary. Don't assume you will get what you want until you actually have it.

The Dog and His Treat 50
One day, Farmer Jones gave <u>Rufus</u> a big treat. Rufus picked up the <u>bone</u>. He trotted off to the <u>river</u>. The <u>dog</u> passed through the gate. One of the <u>geese</u> hissed at him. Next, Rufus walked past a cow in the <u>pasture</u>. The cow called him a "bad dog." Then, the dog passed a flock of <u>sheep</u>. Rufus <u>pretended</u> not to hear the mean words the sheep said. Finally, Rufus reached the <u>bridge</u> over the river. He started across. He saw another dog in the water. That dog had a bigger <u>treat</u>! Rufus was very mad. He <u>barked</u> at the other dog. The bone fell out of his <u>mouth</u>. It hit the water with a big SPLASH! Rufus wanted that <u>bigger</u> bone. He <u>dove</u> at the other dog and into the water. But the other dog was gone!

The Dog and His Treat 51
1. Rufus was greedy, eating the other animals' food. He was also mean. He barked at and chased the geese, nipped the cows' heels, and bit the sheep to get them to move.
2. Answers will vary. The other dog was on his land. The dog wouldn't run away. The dog had a better treat.
3. Answers will vary. People should be satisfied with what they have and not always want more.

A Friend Indeed 55
1 b. Andy's thin legs slipped, and he slid down into the water.
2 b. Andy clung to the leaf and then climbed aboard it like a boat.
3 a. The hunter cried out and the dove heard him.
4 a. Drops of water fell down from the leaves.

Bottom section
Answers will vary.

A Friend Indeed 56
1. Setting: A pond near Andy Ant's home; Characters: Andy Ant, the dove, a hunter
2. Andy knew the hunter was going to try to catch his new friend, the dove.
3. Answers will vary. Andy learned that a kindness can be repaid and even small creatures can do great things.

King Lion 60
A. Greta Goat, B. Tricky Fox, C. King Lion, D. Speedy Sparrow

1. F, 2. T, 3. T, 4. F, 5. T

King Lion 61
1 a. Tricky said he and King Lion talked about the weather and that the king told him that Tricky knew more about the weather than any animal in the woods.
1 b. Tricky said King Lion was a fine fellow, that the king wasn't scary at all, and that they were great friends.
2. Tricky exaggerated to make himself look better, didn't show respect, and wasn't very brave.
3. Tricky learned to respect King Lion and be humble.

Correlations to NCTE/IRA Standards and NAEYC/IRA Position Statement

Partner Read-Alouds: Aesop's Fables supports the National Council of Teachers of English (NCTE) and International Reading Association (IRA) *Standards for the English Language Arts*. This resource also supports the following recommendations from *Learning to Read and Write: Developmentally Appropriate Practices for Young Children*, a position statement of the National Association for the Education of Young Children (NAEYC) and the International Reading Association (IRA).

NCTE/IRA *Standards for the English Language Arts*

Each activity in this book supports one or more of the following standards:

1. **Students read many different types of print and nonprint texts for a variety of purposes.**
   Students read fables plus worksheets related to them while doing the activities in this book.

2. **Students read literature from various time periods, cultures, and genres in order to form an understanding of humanity.**
   The reading passages in *Partner Read-Alouds: Aesop's Fables* are based on classic fables. This book also offers additional literature suggestions.

3. **Students use a variety of strategies to build meaning while reading.**
   Activities in this book support strategies and skills essential to effective reading, such as read aloud with expression and understanding, recall details, sequence events, recognize cause and effect, identify the main character's problem and solution, compare and contrast characters' traits, and make inferences.

4. **Students communicate in spoken, written, and visual form, for a variety of purposes and a variety of audiences.**
   Students speak during partner read-alouds, class discussions, and performances; write words, sentences, and paragraphs; and draw while doing the activities in *Partner Read-Alouds: Aesop's Fables*.

5. **Students use the writing process to write for different purposes and different audiences.**
   Students use parts of the writing process such as prewriting while they write sentences, paragraphs, and stories in this book.

6. **Students incorporate knowledge of language conventions (grammar, spelling, punctuation), media techniques, and genre to create and discuss a variety of print and nonprint texts.**
   While talking about the stories in this resource book and writing their own fables, students analyze the characteristics of this genre and note how punctuation affects oral expression and the meaning of the text.

7. **Students conduct research on a variety of topics and present their research findings in ways appropriate to their purpose and audience.**
   Students research different topics in several activities in *Partner Read-Alouds: Aesop's Fables*.

8. **Students become participating members of a variety of literacy communities.**
   The partner read-alouds, group discussions, and performances in this book help teachers build a classroom literacy community.

NAEYC/IRA Position Statement *Learning to Read and Write: Developmentally Appropriate Practices for Young Children*

The activities in this book support the following recommended teaching practices for primary-grade students:

1. **Teachers read to children daily and provide opportunities for students to read independently both fiction and nonfiction texts.**
   Teachers model reading fables fluently to students and give them the opportunity to read the stories aloud with a partner and to family members. Students also read worksheets to do the activities in this book.

2. **Teachers provide opportunities for students to write many different kinds of texts for different purposes.**
   Students write words, sentences, paragraphs, and stories while doing the activities in *Partner Read-Alouds: Aesop's Fables*.

3. **Teachers provide opportunities for children to work in small groups.**
   Students work in small groups by reading the fable out loud with a partner.

4. **Teachers provide challenging instruction that expands children's knowledge of their world and expands vocabulary.**
   Partner Read-Alouds: Aesop's Fables expands student vocabulary by presenting story-specific words to students.